I0440735

Productivity

BIG Ideas
From The Top 10 Books

By Oran Kangas

1st Print Edition, April 2013

© Copyright 2013 by Oran Kangas

All rights reserved worldwide. No part of this book may be reproduced or given away in any form, without the prior written consent of the author, except for the inclusion of brief quotations in a review.

Legal Notices & Disclaimers:

This book has been thoroughly researched and is designed to provide accurate information. However, that information is current only up to the print date. The author and publisher cannot be held responsible for errors, inaccuracies or omissions, or for the use or misuse of its information.

No part of this book is considered to be legal or financial advice.

This information is presented for educational and entertainment purposes only.

Table of Contents

Preface

The BIG Ideas System is, well, a SYSTEM — a repeatable set of actions that generates a fairly reliable set of outcomes.

Put another way, it's pretty boring to describe. And boring is not a good start ... for a book or a relationship, and I hope we shall enjoy both together.

Yet readers should understand the system "behind the curtain," otherwise they are being asked to rely on the author on blind faith. That is something I have little of myself, and I expect the same is true for you.

So what's a poor author to do? Move the boring stuff to the back of the book, that's what.

So if you are keen to understand exactly why I chose these 10 books over other perfectly good choices, proceed to the back of the ... book for the gory details. I highly recommend you do so, please see the Appendix section.

Let's Get On With It

An ounce of action is worth a ton of theory — Ralph Waldo Emerson

Back already? Oh well, mine not to reason why, mine but to type and cry.

Here's our action plan:

1. Each best-selling book is covered in 1 chapter and a BIG idea is brought forth. Note the dual (and sometimes dueling) goals:

- There is the summary that is not a summary; the review that is not a review. This is more of a revary or a sumiew. The purpose is not to squeeze the author's words down to insignificance or to give you the false impression that you are now the master of the author's domain. Or that I am.

    My goal in that regard is to give you a taste of the author's brew, a whiff of compatibility. To make you more or less likely to pursue further information from that source. There are no affiliate links here. I care not whether you buy their books.

- Then there is the BIG idea section. My guilty secret is that Ideas are my passion. While the idea write-up section is lower in word count than the foregoing section, do not judge an idea's merit by its word count. At last count, the fortunes of 1 company was well into the billions aided by 2 gramatically incorrect words "Think Different."

2. With 10 such books, that makes for <pauses for calculator> 10 chapters.

3. Chapter 11 is my/our Creativity Toolkit, which is immediately put to the test in ...

4. My favorite part, chapter 12. Just yours truly wrestling those 10 topical topless tips into order, armed with nothing but 5 simple creativity techniques.

5. When the digital dust dissipates, there will stand 8 brand-new "actions" for you to integrate into your life. A final bonus is Action #9: How to customize any of the above 10 + 8 idea/tips so that they work just right for you.

Those are my goals for this and every book in *The BIG Ideas* series. I look forward to you telling me how close I came to reaching those goals.

I think that is a pretty terrific concept.

What do you think? The voting button is labeled "B-u-y". :)

Buy The Way (sic) (how's that for a seque? Slick or sic(k). Stop me before I pun again.)

If you will keep reading until the end of this book, I have a special gift for you: a FREE book. The second book of the *BIGideas* series. After a double helping, you will be abuzz with productivity ideas.

Introduction

Productivity is never an accident. It is always the result of a commitment to excellence, intelligent planning, and focused effort. — Paul J. Meyer

Subject

Of the many areas within self-help, I chose productivity for this, the first book in *The BIG Ideas* series, because it is a fairly universal need.

Productivity at work, at home, and on the internet all yield a precious product: saving your time. If you find yourself consistently running out of time, but not worthy projects to spend time on, read on.

I certainly need more productivity in order to write all these books.

We all have the same number of hours in a day, week, or year. Why do some people produce astounding feats with those hours and others have nothing to show? There are several factors, but the one ultimate achievement limiting factor is *time usage*.

There are 2 ways to address that limitation:

1. Buy someone else's time

2. Learn to use yours more effectively.

The first method has some distinct disadvantages. It is expensive, and you have to use up even more of your time to train and supervise. While that is possible, the more direct path is to train and supervise the one person who is always with you.

The second method requires a laughably small expense: get a good book on Productivity. I happen to know of one, if you are interested. Then it is ATA all the way.

ATA

Absorb. Think. Apply.

I am certain that you can do all 3.

A quick word on Absorb: reading is not enough. To passively read is to guarantee failure. You will forget almost everything within a few days. You must absorb the information: internalize it, make it yours.

To insure that your effort will pay for itself hundreds of times over, I have chosen some excellent seed material (some call them books).

So, without further ado (or adont), I present ...

The Top 10 Books

(in alphabetic order):

1. *Brain Rules: 12 Principles For Surviving And Thriving At Work, Home & School* by John Medina

2. *Do More Great Work: Stop the Busywork. Start the Work That Matters.* by Michael Bungay Stanier

3. *Getting Organized: Improving Focus, Organization & Productivity* by Chris Crouch

4. *Getting Things Done: The Art Of Stress-Free Productivity* by David Allen

5. *Lifehacker: Guide To Working Smarter, Faster & Better* by Adam Pash & Gina Trapani

6. *Power of Full Engagement* by Jim Loehr & Tony Schwartz

7. *Tell Your Time: How to Manage Your Schedule So You Can Live Free* by Amy Lynn Andrews

8. *The 80/20 Principle: The Secret to Achieving More with Less* by Richard Koch

9. *The Now Habit: A Strategic Program for Overcoming Procrastination and Enjoying Guilt-Free Play* by Neil Fiore

10. *Time Warrior: How To Defeat Procrastination, People-Pleasing, Self-Doubt, Over-Commitment, Broken Promises & Chaos* by Steve Chandler.

Are you ready to become more productive? Let's get this idea-wrangling rodeo started.

1

Brain Rules:

12 Principles For Surviving And Thriving At Work, Home & School

By John Medina

If you wanted to create an education environment that was directly opposed to what the brain was good at doing, you probably would design something like a classroom. If you wanted to create a business environment that was directly opposed to what the brain was good at doing, you probably would design something like a cubicle. And if you wanted to change things, you might have to tear down both and start over. — John Medina

Quick Summary

Our brains have changed little from those of our forebears, thousands of years ago. There are many active mechanisms that seldom, if ever, are relevant to our current environment.

Those saber-toothed tiger reflexes that kept our ancestors alive long enough to become our ancestors, do not work out so well in the boardroom. Or the bedroom.

This is especially true when it comes to finely tuned skills and behavior patterns required for complex actions, such as in productivity.

Coming from a molecular biologist's perspective, Medina's description of brain functions and disfunctions is quite interesting. He has packaged the information expertly into 12 Rules.

There is a great deal of information that has direct application to education. In fact, that is Medina's passion. His next book was about how to improve learning for babies.

He covers energy, exercise, and sleep **needs** — and their effects on cognitive skills. Ignore this and you will have an unhappy and malfunctioning brain.

He discusses actual differences between male and female brains — and consequences. No wonder the sexes don't understand each other. Our brains are hardwired to process the same data differently!

Is your memory giving you problems?

Do you have stress in your life?

It's all in your head!

But the good news is the brain is capable of learning, changing, and adapting. Not completely, but enough that each of us is totally unique.

At least until we hear a bump in the night.

Concerns About **The Book**

There are only 2 *possible* drawbacks that I noticed. I say possible because some people might find them annoying. I didn't ... at all. They are actually design features the author fully intended.

1. This is not a hard science approach

2. The information is broken up with lots of anecdotes.

What's The BIG Idea?

☑ **Multitasking is physically impossible.**

The human brain is wired to focus on one thing at any given moment. The brain's equivalent of a CPU (Central Processing Unit for the geekically challenged) is sequential, multitasking requires parallel.

Multitaskers just switch attention rapidly between tasks. They should be called *multiswitchers* or perhaps *task-hoppers*.

But instead of gaining anything, each hop is a loss of productivity. The brain must reload data about its "new" task ... every time.

Therefore, to maximize your productivity, **deliberately** focus on precisely one thing at a time.

Conclusion

I thought it was a terrific book. Well researched, well written, and very informative.

What else is in the book? Take a look:

Table Of Contents

long-term memory

Rule #6: Remember to repeat

If you don't repeat this within 30 seconds, you'll forget it ~ Spaced repetition cycles are key to remembering ~ When being underwater could help you remember something

sleep

Rule #7: Sleep well, think well

The brain doesn't sleep to rest ~ Two armies at war in your head ~ How to improve your performance 34 percent in 26 minutes ~ Which bird are you? ~ Sleep on it!

stress

Rule #8: Stressed brains don't learn the same way as non-stressed brains

Stress is good, and stress is bad ~ A villain and a hero in the toxic-stress battle ~ Why the home matters to the workplace ~ Marriage intervention for happy couples

sensory integration

Rule #9: Stimulate more of the senses

Lessons from a nightclub ~ How and why our senses work together ~ Multisensory learning means better remembering ~ What's that smell?

vision

Rule #10: Vision trumps all other senses

Playing tricks on wine tasters ~ You see what your brain wants to see, and it likes to make stuff up ~ Throw out your PowerPoint ~ Pictures are simpler

gender

Rule #11: Male and female brains are different

Sexing humans ~ The difference between little girl best friends and little boy best friends ~ Men favor gist when stressed; women favor details ~ A forgetting drug

exploration

Rule #12: We are powerful and natural explorers.

Book Stats

General Info:

- **Publication Date**: 07/6/2010

- **Publisher**: Pear Press

- **Reviews**: 289

- **Stars**: 4.5

- **Pages**: 301

- **File Size in KB**: 775

- **Reading level:** n/a

Book Identification:

- **ISBN-10:** 0979777747

- **ISBN-13:** 978-0979777745

- **ASIN:** B00AZ8NC0M

Likes:

- **Hardcover:** 0

- **Paperback:** 210

- **Kindle**: 76

Amazon Sales Rank:

- **Hardcover:** 58,546

- **Paperback:** 2,235

- **Kindle**: 5,517

Price:

- **Hardcover**: $11.98

- **Paperback**: $10.20

- **Kindle**: $9.58

- **Audiobook:** $22.36

Meanwhile, our next BIG idea comes from ...

2

Do More Great Work:

Stop The Busywork. Start The Work That Matters.

By Michael Bungay Stanier

(With Seth Godin, Michael Port,

Dave Ulrich, Chris Guillebeau & Leo Babauta)

Because we're in a hurry, we often just grab the first half-decent idea that comes along, regardless of whether it's the best idea we could have. I call this 'first-idea-itis'. — Michael Bungay Stanier

Quick Summary

There are 3 classes of Work (with a capital W):

1. Good (productive work that you are reasonably good at)

2. Bad (stuff that is not worth doing)

3. Ugly (kidding). Great! (making a significant impact).

We all have ToDo lists. One huge problem with them is they consist of Goods and Bads. Greats rarely make it and if they do, they are quickly swamped by the more trivial and mundane Goods and Bads.

The author wants *Great* from us. And he clearly points the way with 15 pointed exercises to help drag the necessary information from your buried memories into the light of day.

However **you** choose to define Great Work, this book will guide you to your unique path.

Inspire someone today: start with yourself.

Concerns About **The Book**

I found it so blindingly good that I could not see any minor faults that *might* have been there.

What's The BIG Idea?

☑ 1 + 2 = Great ToDo List.

Since ToDo lists are notoriously poor for dealing with Great tasks, it's time for a tweak.

Once you have a Great project in mind (and it could be "Find My Great Project"), so no slacking:

1. Break it into bite-sized chunks

2. Write chunk #1 at the top of your ToDo list

3. Choose 2 more chunks of greatness

4. Write them somewhere on your ToDo list

5. The first ToDo is a Must Do. Start there every day

6. The other 2 are Optional Greatness. If you get to and through them, Great. If not, no worries.

Conclusion

By defining your own Great Work, and working it daily, you will inevitably make progress. And by your own definition, it will be significant and meaningful. How do you think that will make you feel?

Might I hazard a guess? Great?

What else is in the book? Take a look:

Table Of Contents

Book Stats

General Info:

- **Publication Date:** 2/22/2010

- **Publisher**: Workman Publishing Company

- **Reviews**: 133

- **Stars**: 4.8

- **Pages**: 200

- **File Size in KB**: 829

- **Reading level:** n/a

Book Identification:

- **ISBN-10:** 0761156445

- **ISBN-13:** 978-0761156444

- **ASIN**: B003HMOW8E

Likes:

- **Hardcover:** n/a

- **Paperback:** 168

- **Kindle**: 16

Amazon Sales Rank:

- **Hardcover**: n/a

- **Paperback:** 33,365

- **Kindle**: 21,453

Price:

- **Hardcover**: n/a

- **Paperback:** $9.47

- **Kindle**: $8.69

- **Audiobook:** n/a

Meanwhile, our next BIG idea comes from ...

3

Getting Organized:

Improving Focus, Organization & Productivity

By Chris Crouch

Certain personality traits may have a significant influence on your ability to become more focused, organized and productive. It is not a matter of any particular trait being good or bad, it is more a matter of whether or not the traits are a good match or a bad match for what you are trying to do. — Chris Crouch

Quick Summary

Presented as "Simple solutions to common productivity issues" it lives up to that.

It is clearly written and has some fresh ideas. It is a collection of ideas that you can easily take or leave on an individual basis. Whether that is a good thing or a bad thing is up to you.

I'm a systems guy, so I would have preferred more organization to the organization info. But that's just my preference, so I'm not marking it as a weakness, merely a *feature*.

Concerns About The Book

- Designed for an office worker situation

- This is not a book weakness, but an alert of sorts. In reviewing the Amazon reviews, I was struck by a singular fact — a huge number of 5-star reviews came from people who attended a *seminar* that the author leads. Apples and oranges, anyone?

What's The BIG Idea?

☑ See your desk.

Everyone works from a desk of some sort. If yours is overflowing in stuff, it will wear on you. Every time you look up, you are reminded of how far behind you are.

Clear the clutter on this key area to clear your mind for more productive work.

There are a multitude of "clutter" books on the market. (Surprisingly they are all anti-clutter. Where are the pro-clutter books? Let's have some balance to the debate. :)).

I chose "see your desk" as the idea because it is more concrete and hence actionable than the analogous "avoid clutter" idea.

The author has a filing system that will help. It is too paper-centric for my taste. But anything that lets you "see the wood" is a step well spent.

Conclusion

This book is well worth acquiring. You are certain to find

something of help to you right away. A future read will likely find other gems that were not right for you first time around.

What else is in the book? Take a look:

Table Of Contents

Gathering Incoming Items

The Five Decisions

The Five Decisions - Discard

The Five Decisions - Delegate

The Five Decisions — Take Immediate Action

The Five Decisions — Put in a Reference File

The Five Decisions — File for Follow-up

Control Point Drawer

Files - Labeled "1" to "31"

Files - Labeled "January" to "December"

Files - Follow-up Forms

Files – People

Files – Meetings

Files – Casual Reading

Files – Waiting for Response

Other Files to Help You Follow Up

Capturing Incoming Items

Back-filling Your 1 to 31 Files

Prioritizing Your Workload

Prioritizing Your Workload – Special Situations

One Thing at a Time

Book Stats

General Info:

- **Publication Date:** 5/29/2010

- **Publisher**: Dawson Publishing

- **Reviews**: 47

- **Stars**: 4.7

- **Pages**: 178

- **File Size in KB**: 247

- **Reading level:** n/a

Book Identification:

- **ISBN-10:** 0975868098

- **ISBN-13:** 978-0975868096

- **ASIN**: B003OIC74W

Likes:

- **Hardcover:** n/a

- **Paperback:** 36

- **Kindle**: 20

Amazon Sales Rank:

- **Hardcover:** n/a

- **Paperback:** 83,392

- **Kindle**: 64,056

Price:

- **Hardcover**: n/a

- **Paperback**: $15.95

- **Kindle**: $9.99

- **Audiobook:** n/a

Meanwhile, our next BIG idea comes from ...

4

Getting Things Done:
The Art Of Stress-Free Productivity
By David Allen

Your mind is for having ideas, not holding them. — *David Allen*

Quick Summary

Allen has sold hundreds of thousands of copies of this book, which has been a best-seller for over 10 years and counting, for a very good reason. He has a very good system which, if used, will make anyone more productive.

The Getting Things Done (GTD to insiders) method relies on writing down all the stuff in your head (which creates stress, not action) and turning the now visible notes into action steps. This lets you focus on taking action, instead of worrying about forgetting something important.

This is primarily a System of mini-systems. The GTD System is composed of these smaller eco-systems:

- The general "flow" of things you deal with (called workflow) — Allen uses a 5 step mini-system

- Project planning — 5 steps mini-system

- Getting started — 3 items (not really a system, just a discussion)

- Cleaning up — gathering (2 steps) and clearing (6 steps)

- Organizing for productivity — make categories, review weekly, keep on top of things, avoid over-commitment, focus on next-actions

- That's it, in a teeny, tiny nutshell.

Concerns About The Book

1. Fluff — lots

2. Repetition — lots

3. Self-promotion — lots, a triple play!

4. Its age is showing: the systems are paper oriented. But then, so are many humans at this time.

What's The BIG Idea?

☑ **Create (and use) a Trusted System.**

Problem #1: The brain is poor at storage and retrieval.

Solution to #1: Therefore, we should externalize such functions when possible. A simple way to do that is: write it when you think it.

Problem #2: The brain, rightfully, does not trust us with such an important task. It is too easy, and common, to write it down and misplace it, spending hours looking for that scrap of paper. Sound familiar?

Solution to #2: Create a single comprehensive system of storing information, so that you will know exactly where to retrieve it. And then **always use that system.**

Once your brain accepts the new way as a Trusted System, it will let go of information more willingly and you can both relax, knowing that important, and not-so-important, matters will be handled at the proper time.

Conclusion

When you think about it, it really makes sense.

1. Write it

2. File it

3. Find it

4. No worries.

But until you have a Trusted System in place, #2 (File it) is the missing link. And all the rest comes crashing down.

What else is in the book? Take a look:

Table Of Contents

Part 1 - The Art of Getting Things Done

A New Practice for a New Reality

Getting Control of Your Life: The Five Stages of Mastering Workflow

Getting Projects Creatively Under Way: The Five Phases of Project Planning

Part 2 - Practicing Stress-Free Productivity

Getting Started: Setting Up the Time, Space, and Tools

Collection: Corralling Your "Stuff"

Processing: Getting "In" to Empty

Organizing: Setting Up the Right Buckets

Reviewing: Keeping Your System Functional

Doing: Making the Best Action Choices

Getting Projects Under Control

Part 3 - The Power of the Key Principles

The Power of the Collection Habit

The Power of the Next-Action Decision

The Power of Outcome Focusing.

Book Stats

General Info:

- **Publication Date:** 12/31/2002

- **Publisher:** Penguin Books

- **Reviews**: 798

- **Stars**: 4.3

- **Pages**: 288

- **File Size in KB**: 688

- **Reading level**: Ages 18 and up

Book Identification:

- **ISBN-10:** 0670899240

- **ISBN-13:** 978-0142000241

- **ASIN**: B000WH7PKY

Likes:

- **Hardcover:** 11

- **Paperback:** 803

- **Kindle**: 55

Amazon Sales Rank:

- **Hardcover**: 18,595

- **Paperback**: 149

- **Kindle**: 1,081

Price:

- **Hardcover:** $15.84

- **Paperback:** $10.50

- **Kindle**: $12.99

- **Audiobook:** $16.50

Meanwhile, our next BIG idea comes from ...

5

Lifehacker:

Guide To Working Smarter, Faster & Better

By Adam Pash & Gina Trapani

You are building your reputation — your brand — one response at a time —
Adam Pash & Gina Trapani

A Quick Summary

If you regularly visit the Lifehacker website, this is not for you. Otherwise, it is. Quick enough?

Okay, assuming you are not in the regular website visitor category, I'll tell you more.

First, go visit the site, at your convenience. It is excellent.

Second, what is a Lifehacker? Someone who intelligently uses technology to make their life better. So basically 2 groups: geeks (who are no longer reading this) and you personal productivity adepts.

The book is a recap of their website. It is filled with dozens and dozens of creative tips, tricks and methods that apply efficient pieces of technology to efficient living.

Technology can be a time-sucking monster or your best ally. This book makes the latter far more likely.

Concerns About The Book

I think they sometimes turn a virtue into a vice with too much detail. Installation instructions are an example.

- You are unlikely to buy the majority of their recommendations

- If you do, instructions are in the box (perhaps written in Chinglish)

- The book instructions may be obsolete by the time you buy and read the book, and buy and need instructions. That is what the blog is for — timely updates.

What's The BIG Idea?

☑ **Have a ubiquitous note-taking inbox.**

Extra points for a BIG word in a BIG idea.

Instant idea capture is essential for maximum productivity. Cocktail napkins don't cut it.

You need a dependable way (David Allen would call it a Trusted System) to capture and collect those nuggets of future greatness. If you can have it computerized from the start, so much the better. (Ever try to decipher a million dollar idea scribbled down in haste, in vain? Maddening).

The central point of their system is found at
http://simplenote.com

And best of all it's a budget friendly price of ... free.

With this system in place, wherever you get that big idea, jot it
down. Into your desktop computer at home, your laptop at the
airport, your ipad on the couch, or your phone at the bar. All
other devices are synched authomatically. On second thought,
maybe those bar ideas belong on a cocktail napkin, along with the
waitress's phone number.

Conclusion

For technophobes, this is a must buy. For technophiles, it's
probably an already have (either the book or the website version).

If you are in the middle, quit straddling that fence; the wonders
of technology await.

What else is in the book? Take a look:

Table Of Contents

Hack 119: Share a Single Printer Between Computers

Hack 120: Optimize Your Dual Monitors

Hack 121: Control Multiple Computers with a Single Keyboard and Mouse.

Book Stats

General Info:

- **Publication Date:** 6/28/2011

- **Publisher**: Wiley

- **Reviews**: 34

- **Stars**: 4.6

- **Pages**: 507

- **File Size in KB**: 8,763

- **Reading level:** n/a

Book Identification:

- **ISBN-10:** 1118018370

- **ISBN-13:** 978-1118018378

- **ASIN**: B0055AUGG8

Likes:

- **Hardcover:** n/a

- **Paperback:** 145

- **Kindle**: 25

Amazon Sales Rank:

- **Hardcover:** n/a

- **Paperback:** 4,102

- **Kindle**: 32,491

Price:

- **Hardcover**: n/a

- **Paperback**: $18.99

- **Kindle**: $16.49

- **Audiobook:** n/a

Meanwhile, our next BIG idea comes from ...

6

Power Of Full Engagement

By Jim Loehr & Tony Schwartz

The most important role of rituals is to insure an effective balance between energy expenditure and energy renewal in the service of full engagement —Jim Loehr & Tony Schwartz

Quick Summary

The framework of the book is: we are not machines, so we have to take care of our bodies in order to be productive. Or to be much of anything.

The obviousness of that can be off-putting. "Of course!" I felt like shouting.

Not an auspicious beginning.

However, the authors quickly won me over, with some "therefores" that were not so obvious.

By the end I was a fan not only of the book, but the authors methodology. Which can also be stated rather simply:

1. Break the complex into simple parts.

2. Analyze and **improve the parts**.

3. When the parts are improved, the system works better.

Obvious, but effective.

The gold in this book comes from improving, sometimes optimizing, daily habits. Since they have dug up the gold, our job is to collect the nuggets and cash them in.

Stripped of the prospector metaphor, the authors present many concrete suggestions for habits to develop, all we have to do is implement.

Increased personal productivity is but a few habits away.

Concerns About The Book

The fundamental principles of the book are very simple, almost simplistic. The authors did well in creating important lessons where many would have been blinded by the obviousness of the fundamentals.

There's a lesson for all of us there. If you missed that lesson, let me make it clearer: sometimes obvious and simple are a good idea to start from.

What's The BIG Idea?

☑ **Decide how you will spend your next time slot: be productive OR rest.**

You are wasting your time to go at anything, if you will pardon the expression, "half-assed."

Go big or go home, as the saying goes.

Go flat out in productive mode, or totally rest up, so you will be ready to go productive.

I apply that by periodic evaluations of my mental state. If I am getting too tired to think clearly, I take a break and then go back to work refreshed or take a nap ... and then go back to work refreshed. Working from home is a definite plus for this strategy.

Conclusion

I had a hard time settling on 1 BIG idea — I had to choose between 4! Count me impressed.

What else is in the book? Take a look:

Table Of Contents

Spiritual Energy: He Who Has a Why to Live

Part Two: The Training System

Defining Purpose: The Rules of Engagement

Face the Truth: How Are You Managing Your Energy Now?

Taking Action: The Power of Positive Rituals

The Reengaged Life of Roger B

Resources

Summary of the Corporate Athlete Full-Engagement Training System

Organizational Energy Dynamics

Most Important Physical Energy Management Strategies

Glycemic Index Examples

The Corporate Athlete Personal Development Plan of Roger B

The Corporate Athlete Personal Development Plan Worksheet.

Book Stats

General Info:

- **Publication Date:** 2/10/2003

- **Publisher:** Free Press

- **Reviews:** 141

- **Stars:** 4.4

- **Pages**: 256

- **File Size in KB**: 1364

- **Reading level:** n/a

Book Identification:

- **ISBN-10:** 0743226747

- **ISBN-13:** 978-0743226745

- **ASIN:** B000FC0SWS

Likes:

- **Hardcover:** 9

- **Paperback:** 75

- **Kindle:** 8

Amazon Sales Rank:

- **Hardcover:** 130,699

- **Paperback:** 7,675

- **Kindle:** 11,810

Price:

- **Hardcover:** $18.48

- **Paperback:** $10.87

- **Kindle:** $9.99

- **Audiobook:** $19.47

Meanwhile, our next BIG idea comes from ...

7

Tell Your Time:

How To Manage Your Schedule So You Can Live Free

By Amy Lynn Andrews

Many time management techniques do a good job of helping you organize your activities. Few challenge you to think about whether you should be doing those activities In the first place. — Amy Lynn Andrews

Quick Summary

This is a good book ... for those who have not read a book on the subject before. If you have, be prepared to be ... reminded ... a lot.

There are lots of tips — and that is, I think, part of the problem. In going for quantity, the author crosses the line into the obvious. Furthermore, simultaneously aiming for quantity and brevity is counter-productive. To the degree that both goals are achieved, quality of ideas must suffer.

The book is well-written, I will grant that. And motivational, another plus.

Concerns About The Book

1. Short, concise, succinct, simple, simplified. I could go on, but then I'd risk being longer than the book itself. Brevity is a good thing. But you can be too brev (sic).

2. Nothing really new on the subject in this book

3. Pushing *personal* religious beliefs repeatedly on a topic *unrelated* to religion in an already too short book is questionable. To be clear, I am not questioning religion, only unlabeled, unsuspected, unrelated, **content**. *Time Management: A Christian Perspective* would be a more accurate and acceptable title. The reader should be advised *before* purchase of any strong orientation.

What's The BIG Idea?

☑ **Downloadable forms can be used to enhance a product.**

Some people have a problem printing from the Kindle. Being able to download useful forms is handy. That actually encourages the reader to follow directions and do the exercises on paper while reading the text. When the book is finished, so is your written plan.

Forms are often "put off" until the reader finishes the book. And by then, they are forgotten. So the written plan an author meticulously created to help the reader, comes to naught. As does the time spent reading.

As an example of this, I have created just such a device

summarizing all the points of this book. I call it a Cheat-Sheet and you will find the link at the back of this book.

Downloadable forms can take almost any form: a report, list, pdf, word document, picture of your cat, your banking account information (just checking to see if you are awake), mind map, audio file, video, etc. You just need a website to place it on (which is far beyond the scope of this book).

Note: I have commented elsewhere in this book (in the Appendix) on how "big" this idea is. So if you find it underwhelming, hold on.

Conclusion

I think this is one of the weaker titles on the subject. I only covered it because my protocol said it should be covered. But we are all different in needs and backgrounds we bring to a book.

This one does have many 5-star ratings. I wondered about that, so I checked the author's website and found that she has affiliates for the book. Connection?

What else is in the book? Take a look:

Table Of Contents

Two Time Management Principles to Adopt

Where Are You Stuck?

4 Steps to Making a Schedule that Works

- Step 1: Purpose

- Step 2: Plan

- Step 3: Place

- Step4 : Plot

Follow Through

About the Author

Personal Note

Printables

- Roles

- The Grid

- Weekly Schedule.

Book Stats

General Info:

- **Publication Date:** 7/27/11

- **Publisher**: Self

- **Reviews**: 105

- **Stars**: 4.6

- **Pages**: 46

- **File Size in KB**: 395

- **Reading level:** n/a

Book Identification:

- **ISBN-10:** n/a

- **ISBN-13:** n/a

- **ASIN:** B005F0H7BK

Likes:

- **Hardcover:** 0

- **Paperback:** 0

- **Kindle**: 44

Amazon Sales Rank:

- **Hardcover:** n/a

- **Paperback:** n/a

- **Kindle**: 5,529

Price:

- **Hardcover**: n/a

- **Paperback**: n/a

- **Kindle**: $2.99

- **Audiobook:** n/a

Meanwhile, our next BIG idea comes from ...

8

The 80/20 Principle:
The Secret To Achieving More With Less
By Richard Koch

A minority of causes, inputs, or effort usually lead to a majority of the results, outputs, or rewards — Richard Koch

Quick Summary

A killer concept in 1897. And truer than ever now.

2 key concepts here:

1. 20% good. This refers to your effort: 20% will produce 80% of the benefit. To work for less is silly.

2. 80% bad. The flip side of the coin. 80% of your time, effort, or whatever measuring stick you want to use, leads to a quarter of the benefits of the first group.

"Yeah, whatever," you say? Nay, I say, pay close attention,

grasshopper.

This applies to everything in your life! This book enumerates ways you haven't thought of.

Grasp this in your 20s and prosper. Ignore it and wake up to a breakfast of Kibble in your 80s.

It's not often that a universal principle is discovered, so show some respect, please.

Concerns About The Book

1. The author repeatedly repeats himself, repetitively. Then there are the redundant parts.

2. More examples would have gone far to fix the above. One would think that in 13 years the author could have come up with a few more. Perhaps he is saving them for the big Kindle release ... in 2080.

What's The BIG Idea?

☑ **Focus your energy on the 20%ers.**

On every important task (and most not-so-important ones):

1. Stop and Analyze: is it a stupid 80%er or a smart 20%er?

2. Blow off the 80%ers: delegate, make a form letter, put a FAQ on your website, or just plain ignore it. It's a time-waster, so don't waste time on it, now or ever. This is not procrastination — it is annihilation ... of a whole class of "obligations." Forever.

3. Revel in the 20%ers. Seek them out and go for them with

gusto. Throw everything you have at them until successfully concluded. Then grab those fat, juicy rewards.

Conclusion

While this is literarily, if not literally, a moldy oldie, a deep understanding of this 1 principle can almost overnight make you 4 times more productive. Quit doing stupid-80% tasks and load up on smart-20% tasks. Make your accountant proud and your spouse speechless.

There really aren't any other major *ideas* in *The 80/20 Principle*. But there are other facts, areas to ponder and a historical perspective to help drive home the central tenet. Perhaps that will be of interest to you.

What else is in the book? Take a look:

Table Of Contents

Being Free; 10. Time Revolution

You Can Always Get What You Want

With a Little Help from Our Friends

Intelligent and Lazy

Money, Money, Money

The Seven Habits of Happiness

Progress Regained.

Book Stats

General Info:

- **Publication Date:** 10/19/1999
- **Publisher**: Crown Business
- **Reviews**: 119
- **Stars**: 4.2
- **Pages**: 288
- **File Size in KB**: n/a
- **Reading level:** n/a

Book Identification:

- **ISBN-10:** 0385491743
- **ISBN-13:** 978-0385491747
- **ASIN:** n/a

Likes:

- **Hardcover:** 1

- **Paperback:** 425

- **Kindle**: n/a

Amazon Sales Rank:

- **Hardcover:** 320,815

- **Paperback:** 12,566

- **Kindle**: n/a

Price:

- **Hardcover**: n/a on Amazon

- **Paperback**: $10.88

- **Kindle**: n/a! Are you kidding me? Wake up publishers — this is **not** the 19th century!

- **Audiobook:** $13.49

Meanwhile, our next BIG idea comes from ...

9

The Now Habit:

A Strategic Program For Overcoming Procrastination

And Enjoying Guilt-Free Play

By Neil Fiore

Procrastination is a habit you develop to cope with anxiety about starting or completing a task. It is your attempted solution to cope with tasks that are boring or overwhelming. — Neil Fiore

Quick Summary

The author starts with the Why and How of procrastination, then gets more detailed with self-talk and fears that perpetuate the problem.

Solutions appear in sections on:

- playing (without guilt)

- breaking tasks down

- fine tuning and

- dealing with other procrastinators.

While the book is not at all a full-fledged time management System (like Getting Things Done), it is a fine bag of individual psychological tips and techniques that will definitely help you become more productive by being less procrastinative (sic).

Concerns About The Book

1. Long on fluff

2. Short on actionable, non-recycled information.

What's The BIG Idea?

☑ **Work in a state of flow.**

Flow is when you are so focused on a task that time disappears from your consciousness. You produce effortlessly.

It is a great feeling to realize that you **have been** in flow. During flow, there is no feeling at all. You come out of it and feel surprised at what you have achieved.

It is like taking dictation, without the pesky dictator. I often experience it in writing.

The only downside is re-entry: you sometimes feel foolish when you realize that

    a. it is dark outside and

    b. you have no idea if is evening-dark or early-morning-dark.

I have actually asked my wife the time, then followed up with "am or pm?" That's always good for a strange look.

It's a state with great appeal. Once you visit, you'll always have a "yearn to return."

Conclusion

It is worth reading. If procrastination is your thing, this book will help you lose your thing.

What else is in the book? Take a look:

Table Of Contents

Book Stats

General Info:

- **Publication Date:** 4/5/2007

- **Publisher**: Tarcher

- **Reviews**: 169

- **Stars**: 4.3

- **Pages**: 224

- **File Size in KB**: 698

- **Reading level:** n/a

Book Identification:

- **ISBN-10:** 1585425524

- **ISBN-13:** 978-1585425525

- **ASIN**: B001QNVP7M

Likes:

- **Hardcover:** 0

- **Paperback:** 123

- **Kindle**: 10

Amazon Sales Rank:

- **Hardcover:** 1,327,962

- **Paperback:** 7,149

- **Kindle**: 15,109

Price:

- **Hardcover**: n/a on Amazon

- **Paperback**: $10.19

- **Kindle**: $12.99

- **Audiobook:** $26.98

———————————

Meanwhile, our final BIG idea comes from ...

10

Time Warrior:

How To Defeat Procrastination, People-Pleasing, Self-Doubt,

Over-Commitment, Broken Promises & Chaos

By Steve Chandler

So once I identify the big scary imagined task as a distortion produced by my own worried mind, I want to go small, as small as possible.

What can I do in the next three minutes? — Steve Chandler

Quick Summary

Billed as "revolutionary," it misses that mark. The information is good, just not "the R word."

What is exceptional is the metaphor — it is martial, not boring old business, making the occasional cliche seem new.

The author is good with language, turning a rather mundane *don't procrastinate* message into a "non-linear approach." They are the same thing, but going all non-linear sounds much cooler.

Instead of worrying about time management, you work on your "cognitive style." See? Cool.

I poke fun at the linguistic approach, but it actually serves a concrete purpose: we've all heard the messages before. The author makes them sound different, and darned if that doesn't make you want to listen anew.

"Act in the present" is good advice, no matter how you phrase it. That, I think, is the bottom line with this book: if you look hard, you'll see some old info and be turned off. But if you listen to the warrior language, you'll be lulled into wanting to give it a try.

If you speak Warrior, you'll love it. I do and did.

Concerns About The Book

There is some padding — the book really could have been shorter.

What's The BIG Idea?

☑ **Use idle 3 minutes for beginnings.**

The opening quote gives it away. Beginnings are the Achilles heel of most people. Wasting spare time is an almost universal trait.

If I have an hour to "kill", I will usually be sensible enough to put some thought into how best to use it.

But 3 minutes? Never.

Well, never before reading *Time Warrior*.

The author has brilliantly taken the most useless chunk of time and turned it into a formidable weapon to use against that implacable enemy: inertia.

Now he's got me talking Warrior Talk.

In a paltry 3 minutes we can begin (i.e., make *some* preparatory action). That has a quadruple benefit:

1. It whittles 3 minutes off the time required to complete the task

2. It starts our mind working on the targeted topic far beyond the 3 minutes

3. It creates momentum

4. Perhaps best of all, having begun, it is much easier to continue.

Conclusion

Time Warrior would be a timely purchase. Set your inner Ninja free.

What else is in the book? Take a look:

Table Of Contents

A pessimist is a human joke

Why am I not sticking with my goals?

Get as small as you can, now smaller

Time to change the world

Let's all get drunk on information

Okay, so, Why am I still procrastinating?

Increase your capacity for living NOW

Now let's all stand up and stretch

Replace knowing with choosing

Failure is the ultimate success

Warm up to what you're doing

And the money will follow

Should I just do the whole thing?

Creating your future

Serving is the opposite of pleasing

More ways to kiss the ground

The way of inspiration

Try risking your identity

Notice I am saying warrior, not worrier

Asking the wrong question

Another way to see yourself

Want to know who you are?

How do I make her perfect?

Capture the problem

Redefine the problem

For goodness sake get some help!

Honor something called completion

I'm depressed by other people's suffering

What are people yearning for?

Making good use of hard times

Go to war against distraction

We know what we need to know

What do victims do?

Do you fear death or commitment?

The past as a regrettable thing

Good robot or bad robot?

Forget about your safety!

Purpose transitions you

Produce something new and beautiful

Your problem is not time management

What gets measured gets done

What about the fear factor?

What are the steps I should take to overcome procrastination?

How does a warrior deal with job loss?

There are no boring things in life

The self-employed warrior

How to love putting things off

You can be the author of urgent

Recovering from overwhelm

Willpower or the choosing to begin it?

What if I don't know what I'm supposed to do?

What if things break down?

Creative means you have Plan B

The future consumes time and energy

Learning to welcome everything

Work itself is what inspires us

Are you fearless or brave?

Let your life be a small thing

How functional is inspiration?

A warrior brings the light

Time is money and money is time

Creation versus attraction

Childhood fears become adult beliefs

There is no such thing as worthiness

Stop forcing things to happen

Looking for the perfect lover

Well-begun is half-done

Passion to transform your world

A warrior overcoming grief

Why am I always choosing unavailable love partners?

Fighting to remain focused

What's the point of labeling things as "impossible"?

I'm worried about growing old

What if I don't have a life purpose?

What about boredom?

Stay in the moment… Yes, this one

Sing for that good vibration

Don't my goals tie me to the future?

How do I deal with my ego?

How do I learn to trust that there will be abundance?

Why do we hate rich people?

But how do I become creative?

How do I help my children with this?

What if I want to get back at someone?

But what if life is still unfair?

But what about family distractions?

How do I find my project?

Waking up feeling bad?

Stop all that thinking

Earn first and spend later

Use your fifteen minutes

What, exactly, do I want to do?

Stop lying to yourself

How do you make life meaningful?

What will set me free?

Book Stats

General Info:

- **Publication Date:** 8/3/2011

- **Publisher**: Maurice Bassett

- **Reviews**: 104

- **Stars**: 4.3

- **Pages**: 238

- **File Size in KB**: 297

- **Reading level:** n/a

Book Identification:

- **ISBN-10:** 1600250378

- **ISBN-13:** 978-1600250378

- **ASIN**: B004NSV2T8

Likes:

- **Hardcover:** n/a

- **Paperback:** 48

- **Kindle**: 27

Amazon Sales Rank:

- **Hardcover:** n/a

- **Paperback:** 8,253

- **Kindle**: 23,788

Price:

- **Hardcover**: n/a

- **Paperback**: $15.95

- **Kindle**: $8.95

- **Audiobook:** n/a

And now it's time to harvest those 10 BIG ideas and see just what will emerge.

11

The Creativity Toolkit

We shape our tools, and thereafter our tools shape us — Marshall McLuhan

Who Needs Creativity?

Maybe nobody. What? See the next section before proceeding with that lynching, folks.

Who Needs A Creativity Toolkit?

You do, most likely. I do, certainly.

There are a few folks who do not. Most of them flip burgers for a living or are dead.

Computer scientists have been working on artificial intelligence for many decades. Their first problem was they couldn't precisely define how they could tell when they got there. So they hit upon the idea of "If a human can't tell the difference, you are there."

Thus was created the ELIZA program project in 1966. Representing itself as a psychotherapist (in another room), the program "sometimes provided a startlingly human-like interaction."

That is what creativity toolkit techniques do for us, provide a startlingly creative-like product.

The real test is this: apply the techniques, "create" some new business concepts, make a million dollars, then laugh when people ask how you became so creative.

I personally find that having specific techniques make creative efforts easier, faster, and more reliable. They insure that I cover the basic bases and in a (curses!) logical order.

My Creativity Techniques For My Creativity Toolkit

I am going to reveal *my secret* techniques to create new order out of chaos.

When I say "my" I do not mean that I *invented* them. Only that these are the ones I actually *use*.

When I say "secret" I do not mean that no one knows about them. Only that few folks regularly *use* them.

Give them a try and I'll bet you'll find a regular use for them, too.

5 simple ways to generate your own BIG Ideas

My techniques (in the order of typical use):

☑ Reorder The Elements

☑ Group/Combine Similar Elements

☑ Label The Groups

☑ Chunk Down

☑ Chunk Up.

Now I have lots and lots of other techniques. No 5-trick pony am I. But amazingly enough, 5 is all we need for this book.

#1 Reorder The Elements

Rather obvious — just *rearrange* the ideas into *any* different sequence.

Let go of perfection — you probably will change the order again and again.

Just jumble them around and look.

For what? Some grouping of ideas that suggest a commonality to you.

Which leads to ...

#2 Group The Elements

Do some of the ideas seem to fit together? Good, that's grouping.

Also look for a separation, ie. a group of 1. For example if 1 idea doesn't *seem* to fit with anything else, place it at either end of your list of ideas.

Later you will see other connections between some ideas. That often comes from ...

#3 Labeling

Start with any thought that springs up. That is a tentative label. Write it down. Then see which ideas fit that label.

Again don't be afraid to change your mind. Often the words of your label will morph into a more precise fit.

You will see examples in the next chapter. For now, you just need the general concept.

Techniques 1-3 generally go together — you will tend to loop through all 3 steps for several cycles.

Once you feel that some sense of order has appeared or that you are hopelessly stuck, then proceed on, to a totally different pair of tools.

#4 Chunk Up

Chunking is a terrific concept which derives from NLP (NeuroLinguistic Programming), a powerful modern combination of psychology, hypnosis, and language. The basic idea of chunking is that after you perform a behavior many times, the mental pieces blend together in your brain to become a single thought *chunk*.

For example, when you first learned to drive, there were countless little actions necessary to make it happen, and a rather precise pattern. Any deviation was life-threatening. Now, you just get in the car and *drive*. You've Chunked Up.

#5 Chunk Down

But try teaching someone else to drive. Suddenly all your automatic behaviors must be disassembled and verbalized. You must Chunk Down.

Ever experience the telephone hell of a Chunked Up person (say a computer Tech) talking to a Chunked Down person (say you)? He will say do X then Y and be proud of himself for his communications skills.

You at the other end experience this: this is no X key. There is a <shift><alt><ctrl>X. 5 minutes later you 2 have agreed on that fact.

On the Y issue, there is not a single item anywhere that corresponds to the words the Tech used. Instead you are supposed to put your mouse over the word File at the top of your screen, click and hold down the mouse button, then you see a sub-menu (a what?) that has 1 of the Tech's magic words, so you tentatively select it. Only to have a third set of choices thrust at you from the other side! Somewhere in that word salad are several words the Tech mentioned.

You ask if that is it and he says "Yeah, that's what I meant, (under his breath) Moron."

That is an example of poor chunking behavior. Both sides think they are speaking English, but 1 is speaking Chunked Up English (dialect Computerista) and the other speaks Chunked Down English (dialect Luddite).

Why should we care? Being able to easily switch between languages, makes you a better linguist.

Similarly, Chunking fluency will make you appear to be more creative. It's a technique, so purists will argue that you are not really creative, but your boss (and salary) will neither know nor care.

That is a very basic explanation. I encourage you to investigate the Chunking concept further.

With toolkit packed, we are ready to rumble. Ideas beware, we are a lean, mean, idea chomping machine!

12

Putting The Puzzle Together

Originality is nothing but judicious imitation – Voltaire

Here Are The Ideas (In The Order Of Discovery)

1. Multitasking is physically impossible

2. 1 + 2 = Great ToDo List

3. See your desk

4. Create (and use) a Trusted System

5. Have a ubiquitous note-taking inbox

6. Downloadable forms

7. Decide how you will spend your next time slot: be productive OR rest

8. Focus your energy on the 20%

9. Work in a state of *flow*

10. Use idle 3 minutes for beginnings

What Can We Make Out Of That?

Let's open up that Creativity Toolkit. The first thing I see is:

☑ Reorder The Elements

Scan the list of ideas and move some. You are the Lone Rearranger.

You want the ideas to stick together or fly apart. In short to group.

Look at "multitasking" — doesn't seem to fit with anything else, so it belongs at either end (it just happened to already be at the top by chance, so I leave it there).

I will copy it to a new list (for your reading convenience only) see Reordered List below. In real life, I would just cut & paste to move the items in the original list.

Reordered List

1. Multitasking is physically impossible

2. Have a ubiquitous note-taking inbox

3. Downloadable forms

4. Use idle 3 minutes for beginnings

5. Focus your energy on the 20%

6. Decide how you will spend your next time slot: be productive OR rest

7. Work in a state of *flow*

8. Create (and use) a Trusted System

9. See your desk

10. 1 + 2 = Great ToDo List.

☑ **Group/Combine Similar Elements**

"Trusted System" & "Note Taking Inbox" go together.

Grouped List

1. Multitasking is physically impossible

2. Create (and use) a Trusted System

3. Have a ubiquitous note-taking inbox

4. Downloadable forms

5. Use idle 3 minutes for beginnings

6. Focus your energy on the 20%

7. Decide how you will spend your next time slot: be productive OR rest

8. Work in a state of *flow.*

9. See your desk

10. 1 + 2 = Great ToDo List.

So far, this has been rather boring. Let's soldier on.

☑ Label The Groups

Start with whatever thought bubbles up. The group may suggest the label, or the label may create the group. It's a back and forth operation.

My first label was "1-Time Actions" which allowed me to connect "see your desk" with "multitasking. These 2 ideas are more 1 time operations *to me* and the others are frequent activities, which could have been a label, but with 8 members, it had little organizational value *to me*.

I keep emphasizing the "to me" because this entire process is totally unique to each individual. There is no right or wrong, we are just engaging in a bit of "Think Different."

Again don't be afraid to change your mind. Later "1-Time Actions" became "Clear The Decks." Both labels are accurate, but the second is more purpose driven.

"First Great Project" label comes straight from a single idea that immediately picked up hitchhikers.

"Downloadable forms" just wouldn't play nice, but pushing it aside yielded the label "Daily Techniques For Dealing With Individual Tasks" which encompassed 4 items!

Then I simply labeled the last idea standing "A Project (For Other People)".

The new labels and ideas are below.

Labeled List

Clear The Decks:

1. Multitasking is physically impossible

2. See your desk.

Identify Your First Great Project:

3. 1 + 2 = Great ToDo List

4. Create (and use) a Trusted System

5. Have a ubiquitous note-taking inbox.

Daily Techniques For Dealing With Individual Tasks:

6. Use idle 3 minutes for beginnings

7. Focus your energy on the 20%

8. Decide how you will spend your next time slot: be productive OR rest

9. Work in a state of *flow.*

A Project (For Other People)

1. Downloadable forms.

That completes this phase. So, what has been accomplished?

10 single ideas from 10 different sources have been grouped into what might be a decent framework for *productivity* planning (as opposed to the more common *project* planning). With a novel

framework to hang our ideas upon, we can do some Chunky style thinking.

Actions Vs. Ideas

Since we are really getting down to the nitty, let's throw in some gritty.

At the moment we have a pool of 10 rearranged, relabeled ideas. Yawn.

We can easily make variations of them. Yawn.

Let's raise the bar. From Idea Mode to Action Mode.

"Multitasking is impossible" is an idea. A useful idea. A forgettable idea.

If you want your ideas to actually improve your productivity, or anything else, you must take them beyond the idea stage ... into reality. I know, it's a cold, cruel place, but someone has to go there, sometime.

Make some "Multitasking is impossible" signs. Now that's an Idea In Action. Far less forgettable and far more likely to have a positive benefit to yourself and others.

But we can do better than that. Add "post them" to your todo list and we have crossed into multiple actions for an idea, making it more powerful yet.

There is 1 final step: develop a full Idea Action System for multiple actions all strategically aligned for maximal effect.

- Who (can help)?

- Where (to post)?

- When (on your todo list).

- Why? The sooner you train yourself out of this bad habit (of trying to multitask), the more focused and productive you will be.

This is but the first step in clearing your mind of out-dated beliefs. There are lots more to be cleared. Seek and destroy.

The macro picture is this: we are turning a single good idea into a powerful action system. If you didn't notice, that is a textbook case of Chunking UP!

Labeling is another natural form of Chunking Up. As is generalizing.

To cement the distinction between up and down, think of a corporation: the person UP at the top, has the widest, more general picture. Go DOWN the ladder, and people are more specific in their duties and job skills.

For idea creation, we can go either way first. Let's get down.

Chunk Down

The idea label seed was "Clear The Decks" (from Labeled List above). We can Chunk Down to:

☑ Action System #1: "Clear Your Mind And Workspace"

We covered the Multitasking signs part above.

The other half of this action system starts at the desk and expands to the full workspace.

As a point of principle, you can get really detailed now, or paint with broader strokes the full System, detailing as you progress.

To keep this managable I will stay broad.

- Start with the desk surface

- If you have to, place everything on the floor, for a while.

- Once you can *See All Your Desktop,* then replace a few *essential* items

- Expand the de-clutter campaign to your computer, cubicle/office, and home office.

☑ Action System #2: Identify Your First Great Project

This is the perfect time for Great Project thinking. You are no longer overwhelmed by stacks of papers on your work surface. Your stress is lower. You have just won a major productivity battle.

Strike now while your motivation is high.

Unless you have a Great Project idea burning a hole in your pocket, I suggest the following for your First Great Project — **Create A Dual Trusted System**:

1. A ubiquitous note-taking inbox to process all new ideas

2. A comprehensive clutter-handling procedure for all external matters.

3. Implement it using the previously mentioned *1 + 2 Method* of Chapter 2.

Then watch your productivity take off.

☑ Action System #3: Deal With Daily Tasks With Cold Efficiency

Every Project, Great or otherwise, should be broken down into smaller chunks. Everybody knows that.

Those chunks should be broken down into individual actionable tasks lasting less than a day.

This is where this Action System #3 is applied. We have 5 specific techniques in our new arsenal:

When planning your day (probably in some form of a ToDo list) be sure to apply *Focus On The 20%*.

1. First, there should be a big Great Project task sitting at the top of your ToDo list. That should always qualify, even if its action step for today is mundane.

2. Second, you should be eliminating those 80%ers for the time-wasters that they are. If that is a problem for you, make whatever stops you from eliminating time-wasters your next Great Project!

3. At the conclusion of each ToDo item, pause and make a conscious decision to next *be productive* OR *rest*. Set a time limit, if it is a rest period.

   If you are in a workplace environment, you will need to be a little creative. Curling up on the floor for a nap might draw a disapproving scowl or a pink slip. Instead, a walk around the office carrying a sheaf of papers will go unnoticed.

4. The *3 Minute* technique is perfect for starting new tasks, particularly when there is a fear factor involved. You can do anything for 3 minutes. Take a bite out of that apple and see just how bad it tastes. Reality seldom lives up to our fears.

5. The last, but hardly the least, technique is to *Work In A State Of Flow*. That wonderful condition is not controllable, but we can certainly invite it in.

To increase the odds of flow, you need to control your environment.

- Phones off

- Outside noise off

- Visitors forbidden.

You are not to be disturbed unless the house is on fire. Even then, tell the firemen to "keep it down, I'm working!"

Set aside a comfortable chunk of time: 2-8 hours.

Turn all clocks around or off. You cannot experience timelessness if you are sneaking peeks at your watch.

Have all your materials handy.

And go. Perchance to *flow*.

☑ Action #4: If It Doesn't Apply To You, Apply Yourself To It!

[Formerly labeled: "A Project For Other People"]

The hand we were dealt is *Downloadable Forms*.

Website owners and authors could easily use this as a vehicle to:

- Enhance the customer/visitor experience

- Gain sign-ups to a mailing list

- Build a relationship.

But you are probably neither an author nor a website owner. Therefore, what? Look more closely.

You *could become* either one or both. In a matter of weeks.

Can you say, next Great Project?

Before we move on, let's back up this mule train. I am serious in the above statement "You could become"

- an author (in weeks or months). Might that change your life?

- a website owner (in days or weeks). What avenues could that open?

Final Technique: Chunk Up

Rising above the data that generated these labels, we can apply them to a larger context. This is known in NLP talk as chunking up.

☑ Action #5: Remove The Small Things, So You Can Address Big Things

Whatever obstacles are weighing you down need clearing.

- If it is a problem in organization, organize or reorganize.

- Unwanted projects? Delegate, renegotiate, or ignore.

- Poor time management? Get clear on the difference between urgent and important? Then focus on important. Remember 80/20.

You need to be *relatively* uncluttered, so that you can think BIG.

Make sure your "Clearing Project" (ie. this item) is written, tangible, and actionable.

☑ Action #6: Make Creating Great Projects A Process

You will quickly get the hang of doing a Great Project. Then lesser endeavors are just not very exciting. You likely have many Great Projects in your future. Make it easy on yourself with a simple system to enable you to quickly move from 1 Great Project to the next.

Make a list of your:

- Dreams

- Life-time goals

- Bucket list.

Then cross off (temporarily) those that:

- Require financial resources way beyond what you consider possible

- Appear unachievable within the next 6 months.

Put a star in front of any that:

- Will act as stepping stones for other great projects

- Can be accomplished within 1 month (by stretching).

Pick a *starred* item for this time. Notice that you have a ready-made list for next round.

☑ Action #7: Deal With Daily Tasks With Intentional Habits

After a bit of experience, you will find yourself falling into patterns of behavior. For some situations, you will develop a preference to handle them with a specific technique.

That is your choice point. Stop and analyze your motivation. Is your preferred technique better or merely more familiar? Decide carefully.

If your pattern is based on familiarity, stop that pattern immediately and do things differently. Then choose the one that works best for you.

When you have that *effective* system down, actively turn it into a habit. (I have a book coming out in a few weeks that explains precisely how to do that.)

In super concise form, the habit process is:

Cue: the type of situation/task you are facing

Behavior: the physical/mental routine you ALWAYS apply

Reward: is whatever works for you: telling yourself you did a great job, or strutting down the office aisle yelling "Who's the man? I'm the man!," or perhaps a simple cookie will suffice.

To form a conscious good habit, you identify the Cue, write out and practice the new desired behavior, then give yourself the promised reward.

☑ Action #8: Consciously Scan For Interesting, Irrelevant Facts. Then Force Yourself To Use Them

When reading a book, or any other form of information gathering, it is often the case that *some* of the material is a really good idea — for someone else.

It is human nature to instantly skip such irrelevant material. That could be a major mistake.

The breakthrough ideas in most fields have come from outside.

So if you want breakthrough ideas, I suggest that you look *not* where all your peers are looking, but at the *irrelevant* ideas that they skip over.

Say to yourself, "Nobody in my field does that. How could I adapt it to my situation?"

If nothing comes to mind, go ahead and skip.

Just know that a nugget awaits you *somewhere*. But if you do not look for it, you will *over*look it.

It's Time For Action

You now have the original 10 big ideas, plus 8 exciting new actions to apply. You just saw how I did it. If you implement a few at a time, you should experience a jump in your personal productivity.

But you have to do your part. The key word is DO.

There is a tendency among those who love ideas to just think and admire. What a lovely idea that is.

Hogwash. If the idea does not spark action it is worthless ... to you.

Another reason for concentrated action is to know when an idea, technique, process, or system works for you. If it doesn't work, then what?

Customization

If you said "give up on it," then you must stay after school and write on the chalkboard 100 times, "I will not give up!"

This is where you apply a little thought, which should appeal.

How can you change/modify/expand/contract/extract/etc. the idea to get a new working model? That is what this entire long chapter has been about.

I arranged the ideas 1 way, then another, until I got something with potential.

That is exactly what you must do. Use my techniques on your situation. This is customizing the data to fit your unique circumstances. And make no mistake, your circumstances are unique.

☑ Action #9: If Something Does Not Work For You, Customize It

It would be most unusual if every technique worked perfectly for all people in all situations, wouldn't it? "Doesn't work" just means "isn't customized properly."

But you now have the tools to fine-tune — to customize — your results to eventually achieve unparalleled performance.

And by the time you have implemented and customized your productivity techniques, I shall have published the next book in the *Big Idea series* to address another area of your life.

I hope we have a long and fulfilling journey together.

Appendix: **The Method To The System**

We do not see design as a discipline, but as a way of life. We hope we can teach our students to have confidence in a methodology of how to innovate routinely. —— David Kelley

The **BIG** Ideas System is a series of books based on a specific methodology:

1. Minimize

2. Expand

3. Organize

4. Innovate.

Here is how that works.

Minimize To The Max

A popular new trend in ebooks is to summarize a best-seller to save the reader time. That is minimization in action.

We carry that to the extreme by extracting a single "BIG idea" from that best-seller.

That saves even more time, right? It is also less of an ethical conflict, because we do not "spoil the book" by revealing the entire contents. There remain many other good ideas, which the reader is free to investigate. Or not.

That is cool and all, but would make for a mighty short read.

Expand 10X

Next we **expand** that idea to multiple books, in fact the top 10.

So you are getting a BIG idea from the 10 best-selling books on any given subject.

Organize

But wait, there's more.

I will organize those 10 great, but isolated ideas from those 10 great, but probably isolated authors. And create an organized set of big ideas. With greater organization the ideas become:

1. Simpler to apply

2. Easier to remember

3. *Actionable.*

Innovate

As a final sweetener, I will take those freshly organized actionable ideas and innovate.

Something new shall arise from this witch's brew of reconstituted big ideas. What shall it be? I don't know. I haven't gotten there yet.

But you will be peeking over my shoulder the whole way, watching as I try 1 creative technique after another.

Innovation in action: just you, me, and the tightrope. Will I fall and go splat, or will I emerge with a shiny new ... something?

Now we're talking. Well, I'm talking; hopefully you are still listening.

The Triple Selection Process

You may want to know how I arrived at the particular (some might say peculiar) choices that became this book.

Selection 1

First off, I select a subject. Each book in this series will, of course, address different subjects.

I am particularly interested in the general area of self-help for 2 reasons:

1. First, I could personally use a considerable amount of help.

2. Second, no one else has offered, so I guess it is up to me.

Once a subject is chosen, the next hurdle is:

Selection 2

Pick the "top 10" books on the subject. It is difficult to be objective here, so I adopted a procedure.

First I examined the Top 100 (or so) lists from likely suspects, like The New York Times, USA Today and Publisher's Weekly. This proved useless, as there are so few books represented that to find 10 on 1 subject would be a statistical impossibility.

So, it came down to Amazon and Barnes & Noble.

I fully planned to use both. I did the first round of research on Amazon. Then I turned to B&N.

Only to discover that it, predictably, doubled my work, but added ... not a whit to the results.

With a source in hand, it now became a fairly straightforward process.

- search for books and ebooks on the subject

- delete books published within the last 3 months because ranks fluctuate wildly within that time-frame

- sort by Amazon Sales Rank

- select the top 10.

- **Note**: The Sales Rank changes hourly, so if one of your favorites did not make the cut, it might have missed by minutes. Still, this is the most objective method I could think of.

Selection 3

Finally we come to picking the BIG idea. That, I will admit, was quite challenging, and necessarily subjective.

4 characteristics were sought, but not always found:

1. A **personal improvement** element — which ruled out many corporate applications

2. **Useful** to as many people as possible — there went some CEO training ideas

3. **Actionable** — I simply detest conclusions which are vague generalities

4. Some degree of **originality** to it (or at least potential).

NOTE: I am not necessarily looking for the *biggest* idea in the book. Nor necessarily even an idea that appears personally earth-shaking.

What I am seeking is big *potential*. This has a large trade-off, which you need to understand. The best way to explain is with an example.

In Chapter 7 you will encounter a remarkably UNbig idea: Use downloadable forms. That meets practically none of the 4 above characteristics. Yet in Chapter 12 it blossoms into the *potential* for a career-changing, life-changing event.

You can think of this as an example of the Greek proverb "mighty oaks from tiny acorns grow." Or you can file it under "mighty dumb idea."

What Now?

Well that sort of depends ... on whether you're coming or going.

If you are a new reader following instructions, then you'll want to hop back to the beginning.

If you've already read the book and have just moseyed on down here, just keep on moseying down (I love that word).

Cheat-Sheet

Everything In 1 Place

———————————

The price of greatness is a few good habits — Oran Kangas

Your 10 Big Ideas To Experiment With:

1. Multitasking is physically impossible

2. 1 + 2 = Great ToDo List

3. See your desk

4. Create (and use) a Trusted System

5. Have a ubiquitous note-taking inbox

6. Downloadable forms can be used to enhance a product

7. Decide how you will spend your next time slot: be productive OR rest

8. Focus your energy on the 20%

9. Work in a state of *flow*

10. Use idle 3 minutes for beginnings

Your 9 Action Items To Implement:

1. Clear your mind and workspace

2. Identify your first great project

3. Deal with daily tasks with cold efficiency

4. If it doesn't apply to you, apply yourself to it!

5. Remove the small things, so you can address big things

6. Make creating great projects a process

7. Deal with daily tasks with intentional habits

8. Consciously scan for interesting, **irrelevant** facts. Then force yourself to use them

9. If something does not work for you, customize it.

My 5 Customization Techniques:

1. Reorder The Elements

2. Group/Combine Similar Elements

3. Label The Groups

4. Chunk Down

5. Chunk Up.

If you would like a pdf version of this Cheat Sheet, just go to http://bit.ly/10CJLsI for an instant download.

Conclusion

If all the economists were laid end to end, they'd never reach a conclusion —
George Bernard Shaw

That's it, my friends.

10 BIG ideas + 10 best-selling books + 9 actions from me + my 5 processing methods.

What does that add up to? I hope you will do me a favor and answer *that question* in an Amazon Customer Review.

A review is a simple thing that serves the entire public. Just a few words of honesty in a world bereft thereof.

Amazon notices such things and rewards authors accordingly. So whether my "big ideas" and I live in poverty or splendor is in your hands. :)

Best wishes,

Oran

About The Author

Almost anyone can be an author; the business is to collect money and fame from this state of being — A.A. Milne

Oran Kangas

Oran is a researcher and author.

Born in Phoenix AZ, he was quickly whisked away to sunny California, where he has remained ever since.

He attended the University of California San Jose for more years than he cares to remember. "Eventually stumbling out into the real world armed only with 2 pieces of paper: Master's degrees in Psychology and in Physical Education.

"I soon learned that paper doth not a career make. Having no real skill other than classroom sitting, I made a brilliant career choice ... and returned to college. This time computers were the bright shiny object that held my attention ... for the next half century."

Even today Oran spends 12 hours a day, 7 days a week staring at the 1-eyed beast that patiently stares back. The computer and internet are his daily companions.

Oran now lives in Northern California with his other companions: 1 wife and 15 cats.

They operate the nonprofit FIV Cat Rescue (http://fivcatrescue.org/). Their 3 year mission is to prevent the annual slaughter of 1 million cats in the USA alone because of outdated information.

Contact Page

Other Books By Oran

Juicing Joy: Fruits, Berries, & Melons Available now at Amazon.com

Contact Me Online:

I'd love to hear from you. Please drop by for a visit: http://BIGideas-publishing.com

If you'll let me know how this book can be improved, I can make the very next edition better.

Get a FREE Book: Productivity Tips: BIG Ideas From The Top 10 Books

This is not a tiny little free report, like you would expect. It is the full second book in the *BIG Ideas* series. The intellectual equal of the one you just read.

The following books (in alphabetic order) are the Top 10 Books used:

1. *I Used To Be So Organized: Help For Reclaiming Order And Peace* By Glynnis Whitwer

2. *No B.S. Time Management For Entrepreneurs* By Dan Kennedy

3. *Organizing Plain And Simple: A Ready Reference Guide With Hundreds Of Solutions To Your Everyday Clutter Challenges* By Donna Smallin

4. *Out Of The Crisis: The Power To Change Anything* By W. Edwards Deming

5. *SuperCompetent: The Six Keys To Perform At Your Productive Best* By Laura Stack

6. *The 7 Minute Solution* By Allyson Lewis

7. *The Accidental Creative: How To Be Brilliant At A Moment's Notice* By Todd Henry

8. *The Pledge: Your Master Plan For An Abundant Life* By Michael Masterson

9. *The Power Of Less: The Fine Art Of Limiting Yourself To The Essential... In Business And In Life* By Leo Babauta

10. *The Wealthy Freelancer* By Steve Slaunwhite, Pete Savage, & Ed Gandia

To Claim Yours, go to http://BIGideas-publishing.com/

www.ingramcontent.com/pod-product-compliance
Lightning Source LLC
Chambersburg PA
CBHW070536290526
45790CB00002B/518

* 9 7 8 1 4 8 4 0 6 9 7 6 9 *